Those
Funny
Kids!

Those
Funny
Kids!

by Dick Van Dyke

Edited by Ray Parker

Drawings by Phil Interlandi

GEORGE PRIOR
PUBLISHERS
London, England

G.K.HALL&CO.
Boston, Massachusetts
1978

Library of Congress Cataloging in Publication Data
Main entry under title:

Those funny kids!

   Large print ed.
   1.   Teaching--Anecdotes, facetiae, satire, etc.
I.   Van Dyke, Dick.   II.   Parker, Ray.
[LA23.T47 1978]   372.1'1'020207   78-24436
ISBN 0-8161-6650-1

Copyright 1975 © by Dramatic Features, Inc.

Illustrated by Phil Interlandi

Published in Large Print by arrangement with
Doubleday & Company, Inc.

Set in Compugraphic 18 pt English Times

Available for sale in the British Commonwealth from
George Prior Publishers, 37-41 Bedford Row,
London, W.C.1., England

British Commonwealth rights granted courtesy of
Doubleday & Company, Inc.

ISBN (U.K.)   0-86043-316-1

Contents

Contents

Foreword

This is a book about kids and teachers, and all the funny things that really happen in our classrooms. Teachers all over the country sent me thousands and thousands of true-life stories, and the best were selected for these pages.

Like my earlier book, *Faith, Hope and Hilarity,* which told of kids and their hilarious encounters with religious training, this one shows anew the surprising and inventive ways a child's mind works as it begins to cope with the complexities of life.

I had a lot of laughs putting this book together, and I can only hope you have half as much fun reading it. In these pages you may also find occasional bits of childhood wisdom as well as laughter, because children are very perceptive observers, far wiser than we might think.

As the book began to grow, I also found myself drifting back to memories of my own school days.

My favorite pursuit in school, back in Danville, Illinois, was reading. I was a constant, avid reader, so addicted to books that they had me doing sixth grade work in English by the time I reached the fourth grade. But I had a physical problem with writing, because I was left-handed. In those days, it was considered a handicap to write left-handed. And since I was a southpaw, they changed me over in the third grade. We lefties had to learn to write all over again, with our left hands behind us. Of course educators have since learned that changing a left-handed person over can create all sorts of problems, from neuroses to stuttering. But to this day I can't write with my left hand, although I still draw, paint and do everything else with it. It seems ironic that I won a writing award in the Palmer Method of penmanship for neatness with my right hand — and today you can't read my writing.

Besides being a southpaw, I was also the tallest kid in grammar school. By the age of eleven, I was the same height as I am now — six feet-one. I was taller than any of my teachers . . . a real stringbean.

As the tallest, skinniest kid around, I was considered a natural for the basketball team — but I had developed too fast and wasn't very coordinated. I warmed the bench all season and got only one chance to play. I'll never forget that big night. My parents had come to see me star in the game. The moment came when the coach called out, "Van Dyke!" I leaped up, and the seat ripped right out of my trunks!

Besides being tall, I matured early. When I was in the fifth grade, I had to attend eighth grade music classes because I was already a bass. I loved music class and played first trombone in our band in the seventh and eighth grades.

One year our band even made it to the State Finals Band Competition. We were up against Gibson City, and our big number featured a trombone solo — by me. I had to stand up to play it. Well, I really blew it — so bad that I just quit and sat down. We lost the competition, and that ended my career as a musician.

It was fun growing up in a small midwestern town. I didn't know it then, but a couple of my playmates would become nationally known. One was the singer-pianist Bobby Short. He and I started out together in the first grade, when his head barely came to the keyboard.

Gene Hackman is another kid I won't forget. He was four or five years younger than his uncle Bob, who was one of my closest friends.

All of us liked to get together at the big social center, Carson's Drugstore, a block from school. I never had a car, like a lot of kids who had Model A Fords, because I never could save up enough money. But

I did have a prestige job after school at age sixteen, as a disc jockey at the local radio station. I'd play records, read the news and take the station off the air at 11 p.m. Then kids started coming down to sit around the lobby while I played music. Soon they got to dancing, and eventually it became a party, with everybody dancing and drinking cokes. But one night the manager came in and caught us, and that was the end of that piece of midwestern wickedness.

I felt like quite a wheel in my high school years. I was president of the student council in my sophomore year, president of the junior class and vice president of the dramatic club. But then I sloughed off and didn't show up for meetings because of my busy social life. So, in my senior year, another guy beat me out for senior class president by two votes. Mad as I was, I knew I deserved it.

This is as good a time as any for me to make a minor confession — that I am a high school dropout. I had just two credits to go when the war came along. I enlisted in the Air Force and never went back for my diploma. Despite this, it seems hardly necessary to say, I am a strong believer in the best, most relevant education for everyone.

Looking back on the schooling I did have, I recall that my favorite teacher was Miss Miller in English.

An enthusiastic teacher makes all the difference, it seems to me. Naturally it is important for schools to provide adequate and decent facilities and equipment, and to limit classroom size so as to create a learning situation instead of a mob scene. But when all that is done, it still comes down to that solitary human being facing the class. At that moment of truth, I doubt that the various educational theories have all that much to do with results. It is *who* is teaching that counts.

If you think back to your own classroom days, you will probably remember at least one teacher who gave you a basic direction in life. Perhaps that teacher gave you pride in developing some ability that you hadn't known you possessed. Or perhaps that person stuck by you during discouragements until you mastered a difficult problem and gained a new confidence in yourself. Or perhaps, like my Miss Miller, she set your imagination to work and gave you a tantalizing glimpse of that wider world of the human spirit.

Obviously, a good teacher gives far more of herself than mere instruction in a subject. She gives heart and courage, confidence and inspiration to the growing, malleable people entrusted to her care.

Teachers like Miss Miller are still on the job, as my own children can testify. My daughter Carrie Beth had an English teacher, a man she just worshipped, in Portola Junior High in the San Fernando Valley. My two boys had him, and they too came home talking about him. Eventually we met him and became friends. He is a superb human being, full of life and interested in everything, and he transmits this attitude to his students.

Not all teachers are outstanding, any

more than are all doctors, lawyers or anyone else. Teaching can be hard and sometimes discouraging work, especially in today's world of slashed budgets, overcrowded classrooms and vandalism unknown in earlier days. But during the writing of this book, I came to know many teachers in a personal way, as people trying to cope with a job that is sometimes exciting, often routine, almost always challenging and never without surprises.

I enjoyed hearing from people like Sister Grace Melville of the Immaculate Conception Convent in Amenia, New York, who has taught first and second graders for 45 years! She described her typical day as being "like trying to keep 27 corks under the water at the same time."

As Sister Grace might well agree, teaching is not exactly a tranquil, ivory tower kind of existence. Sometimes teachers, being human, get tired and impatient like the rest of us. Then they feel like the woman in Marblehead, Massachusetts who wrote: "The only way I get control of these monsters is with a whip and a chair. Oh well, Parent Conference Day is coming and I'll get my revenge. I've already told one mother that her kid is the worst brat in ten states. She and I are not on very good terms, anyway. She claims that I am 'repressing her boy's natural vivaciousness.' I told her that the next time her kid bites me, I'm sending him home in a cage."

I received all sorts of personal thoughts worth sharing, such as a poem by a retired teacher, Mrs. Maria Macari of Shreveport, Louisiana, who wrote, "Children are sponges who, at length, slowly but surely absorb all your strength, leaving you listless, limp as a sack . . . but just

9

squeeze them tightly and get it all back."

I heard from teachers who really love their work and told me why, like Mrs. Betty Averitte of Fort Worth, Texas. She spoke of "the joy you feel to finally see a non-reader suddenly reading and enjoying a book, or one who couldn't add two and two discovering that math makes sense, is useful and can be fun." And she adds, "Maybe I'm prejudiced, but I think second graders are the beautiful people. They are still naive enough to be perfectly honest, and tell it like it is, whether flattering or not; and young enough to think Teacher knows a little more than they do, and to depend on you. They are also open enough to still give you a hug as they leave each day, or to slip little notes on your desk."

On the lighter side, I remember glimpses of school behind the scenes, such as of a Franklin, Ohio principal, Mr. Manring, who always dons roller skates during the school's Halloween celebration and zooms down the halls in a ghost costume. And I think of another well-intentioned principal, Dr. Barry Herman of New

Haven, Connecticut, who visited one of his teachers in the hospital to cheer her

up. En route he bought a jar of hard candies, not bothering to read the label, and presented them at the teacher's bedside, saying, "Something sweet for a sweet person." The teacher thanked him, then opened the package and said, "But these are sour balls!"

And while this is a light-hearted book, I would like to be serious for one moment and add my voice to those who believe that free public education is the glory of this country. In a society that is frequently labeled materialistic, our highest rewards often seem to go to those who have the lowest ethics. I don't know any teachers who are getting rich in this country, but I've met and heard from a lot of them who seem to care a great deal about our schools and our kids. They give of themselves, out of love for our young and a pride in a great profession. It is to them that I would like to dedicate this book about kids and teachers, with all respect and affection.

As with my previous book, *Faith, Hope, and Hilarity,* I had the help of Ray Parker in gathering this material. I would particularly like to thank him for his efforts and to thank the teachers all over America who were good enough to send me the stories which appear in this book.

Classroom Funnies

Much of the fun in humor depends on surprise — the sudden shock when something totally unexpected happens that makes us laugh. Since a teacher's life is full of surprises, it's no wonder that some of them feel they are living in a situation comedy.

Consider the New York City teacher whose adventure with her second graders sounds like a Woody Allen movie. She took her class on a field trip to the Museum of Natural History, where a highlight of the tour was a replica of the human female form with lights and a recording describing the various parts in sequence. Suddenly the lights and sound went out of sync. And just as the voice was telling about the two vital parts of the body that help us hear, what should light up but the figure's mammary glands. It took teacher the rest of the day to calm down her three dozen seven-year-olds.

In Shreveport, Louisiana, a fourth grader returned to afternoon classes following his grandfather's funeral. The teacher, concerned that the boy might still be upset by the experience, asked him, "Were you very close to your grandfather?"

The boy shook his head back and forth and said, "Oh no, ma'am, he was about fifteen feet across the room from me in a big box."

Because kids love to share whatever is going on at home, teacher is often the first one in town to know what's happening. In Oak Park, Illinois, a kindergartener came into class, tremendously excited. "We have a new baby at our house," she said. "A little sister?" teacher asked. "No." "So you have a baby brother!" teacher exclaimed. The girl's face fell and she said, "Somebody told you."

Another girl came racing into kindergarten in Royal Oak, Michigan, and reported, "My mother just had a new

baby and it was born too soon, so they put it in a percolator."

A teacher in Norwich, Connecticut told her first graders about a woman in the news who had just had five babies at one time. "Does anyone know what having five at once is called?" she asked. One little girl said, "Giblets."

In a pre-school class in Herscher, Illinois, a little girl asked the inevitable question: "Where do babies come from?" But before teacher could answer, another girl volunteered to explain. "When a daddy loves a mommy," she said, "he has this special stuff he gives mommy. She puts it in her tummy and a baby grows up in there, and when it is big enough, mommy goes to the hospital and the doctor takes it out." The teacher was amazed at the girl's mature answer — until a little boy said, "That's not it. Babies are brought by storks." "I know," said the little girl, "but my mommy hasn't learned that yet."

In Eugene, Oregon, a second grader came to class in tears and explained his dog had been killed by a car. After a

moment of symp-
daughter of a taxi
dog to my mom a.
you.''

Children always love
imagine what they will be
up. In Chelmsford, Massach
told the class he wanted to
"What would you do if I can
with a tummy ache?'' asked tea
don't know,'' the boy admitted.
would you do if I had a broken a
Again the boy said, "I don't know.
moment later he added, "Maybe I'd bett
be an engineer.''

Kids always enjoy learning about
various occupations, especially when
someone with that particular job visits the
classroom. In Midvale, Utah, the
pharmacist-father of a pupil visited the
first graders to tell about his profession.
He spent quite a while explaining what
prescriptions were, how he filled them and
what information goes on the bottle
labels. Then he asked for questions. "I

have on
the me

In
grade
ann
doc
"W
kr

17

e," said a boy. "How do you get
icine bottle into the typewriter?"

Brooklyn, a teacher asked her third
rs what they wanted to be, and a boy
unced he was definitely going to be a
tor. "Why?" asked the teacher.
ell," he said, "it's the only thing I
ow."

In Kitchener, Ontario, a first grader
impressed his classmates by saying,
"When I grow up, I'm going to be a lion
tamer. I'll have lots of fierce lions, and
I'll walk in the cage and they'll roar." He
paused a moment, looking at his
classmates' faces, and then added, "Of
course I'll have my mother with me."

A boy in Ranch Palos Verdes,
California also had his future all figured
out. "I want to be a lawyer," he said,
"because I like to argue and I want to get
paid for sitting down, like my dad."

Since America is a melting pot of races
and creeds, teachers sent me a number of

classroom interracial stories — and here are some of my favorites:

A teacher in Bloomfield, New Jersey was explaining the Peace Corps to her students. "Imagine what a couple of native islanders would think at seeing whites in their village for the first time," she exclaimed. A black student grinned at her and said, "There goes the neighborhood."

A black boy in Muskegon, Michigan looked at his white Easter rabbit project and said, "Now this is just what I need — a honky rabbit."

In a New York grammar school where several ethnic backgrounds are represented this exchange took place:

Student #1: "My father comes from Hong Kong and I'm Chinese."

Student #2: "I'm Japanese."

Student #3: "I'm Harlemese."

In a small Minnesota town where practically everyone is of Scandinavian descent, a boy who was an Asian war orphan was absent from kindergarten on the day he had to go to court for his citizenship. Meanwhile the teacher was explaining to the class why little Bobby was absent, and what it meant to be a U.S. citizen. She finished her explanation by saying, "Now he's just like us." A few weeks later, a little girl with golden curls tapped the teacher on the elbow and asked, "When is Bobby's hair going to turn blond?"

Perhaps the zaniest of all such stories came from a Brooklyn teacher who was asked by a Chinese boy, "Are you Italian?" "Yes," she said. The boy turned to a black classmate and said, "I told you — all Italians look alike."

After summer vacation a pre-schooler in Shawnee Mission, Kansas heard his mother explain they had joined a car pool.

One morning en route to school he said, "We've been driving around all week. How come I haven't been swimming yet?"

Another literal-minded youngster in

Kansas City, Missouri was puzzled by a list of supplies the children would be needing for the following term. "It says here that the girls have to wear a one-piece gym suit," he said. "Which piece?"

In San Marino, California, a first grader reported into the school office because she was late. The secretary said, "You're tardy." "No," said the girl, "I'm Diana."

And in Amenia, New York, a teacher gathering information for record cards asked a little girl for her father's name. "It's Archie," the girl said. "Archibald?" asked the teacher. The girl pointed to the top of her head and said, "Just a little bit right here."

Children have a way of *almost* understanding a word and then using it as though they did, like the girl singing the national anthem with this line, "And the rompers they washed were so gallantly streaming."

Another girl was sure she knew what bears did in the winter, telling her teacher, "They vibrate."

A kindergartener in Hamilton, Ontario noticed a storm billowing up outside and said, "It looks like we're going to have a tomato."

In Virginia Beach, Virginia a girl saw

her teacher's record album and asked her to play her favorite selection from the Disney film, *The Sorcerer's Appendix.*

Quite often the mix-up in a child's mind comes when the word sounds like another that is more familiar to him. A Franklin, Ohio teacher offered to teach her

homeroom students to knit as a winter project, and a boy said, "My aunt knows how to knit. She crocheted a big African."

In Los Angeles, a boy returned a

dog-eared history of the Republic of France to a school librarian who wondered aloud, "Isn't this a bit technical?" The boy replied defensively, "It was just like that when I got it."

A bright little girl in Clinton, Wisconsin returned an overdue book and said to the librarian, "Here's the two cents fine. But will you tell me one thing? Can you actually make a living from this?"

In a fifth grade class in Brooklyn, the teacher asked, "Does anybody know what a toboggan is?" The class pondered a while, and finally a boy said, "It's when somebody tries to get something for less money."

A sixth grade teacher in Chester, Pennsylvania was dismayed at the amount of rough language being used in the school yard, so she decided to discuss it with her class. "Does anyone know what profanity is?" she asked. A boy raised his hand. "It's the thing in the bedroom where your mom keeps perfume and jewelry."

Another boy just learning to read startled his teacher after recess in a Springfield, Oregon class by running up to her and reporting breathlessly: "There's a dirty word on the bathroom wall! I know! I sounded it out!"

A boy came home from kindergarten in Shreveport, Louisiana to announce that he had a role in the school play, saying, "I'm going to be the nauseator."

In Cincinnati, a girl surprised her teacher by singing a verse from "Molly Malone": "She was a fish mugger, and that was no wonder, for her father and mother were fish muggers too . . ."

In Coeur d' Alene, Idaho, the class had a project of raising flowers from seed. A girl said, "Let's discuss it tomorrow and I'll ask mom to help us. She's been going to meetings of plant parenthood."

The athletics teacher in Plymouth, New Hampshire was telling the fourth grade

boys what they would need for their gym classes. When he said they should all bring a health supporter, a boy said, "I'll need to bring *two* — because both my knees are weak.''

Living in the coastal California town of Manhattan Beach, a teacher assumed that all children in class could swim by the age of 10. So when a boy admitted he couldn't, the teacher said, ''You mean to tell me that growing up with all that water out there, you can't swim?'' The boy replied, ''There's a lot of air out there and I can't fly, either.''

In Ames, Iowa, a teacher was both impressed and shocked when a boy told her, ''I worked on my English homework until after 12:30 last night.''
''You shouldn't have nearly that much work to do,'' she said. ''What time did you start?''
''Right after the Johnny Carson show.''

An art teacher who entered the classroom in the city of California, Maryland and found the regular teacher wasn't there was reassured by a little girl who said, ''It's okay. I'm the room thermometer.''

My Beast Teacher

Many little kids in kindergarten and first grade believe that their teacher is a special kind of creature who actually lives in her classroom and has been around since time began, like the characters in storybooks. I suppose some explanation for this fanciful idea lies in the words of a poet who described the very young as still "trailing clouds of fantasy." With kids at an age when Santa Claus and the Easter Bunny are as real in their own way as Mom and Dad, why shouldn't teachers eternally dwell in classrooms?

Yet it is often a shock for teachers to find themselves regarded as not quite flesh-and-blood human beings. A teacher in Coulter, Iowa remembers a sizzling August day when she stopped for a drink at the playground fountain. As she straightened up, she found herself surrounded by a dozen first graders with their mouths agape like startled sparrows. One gasped, "Do *teachers* get thirsty, too?"

Many youngsters aren't even aware that teaching is a job. Discussing after-school activities, a teacher in Shawano, Wisconsin told her first graders, "When I get home from work, I like to sew." A boy looked surprised and said, "Where do you work?"

A kindergarten boy in Alhambra, California asked his teacher, "Do you sleep on the rug at night?" She smiled and said "No." The boy turned to his little brother and said, "See? I toldja she slept on the tables."

(I must confess I thought the same thing when I was a little kid. It always used to stun me to see a teacher on the street, away from her classroom. I guess I thought she just popped out of a closet every morning when school began.)

Another teacher, rather frazzled by a hectic day, was disconcerted when a girl asked where she "worked," and replied, "This is it — teaching."

The girl said, "You mean you get *paid* for this?"

An older and somewhat wiser second

grader was certain that teachers get paid. He reasoned this way: "I'll bet they wouldn't be here if they didn't."

As many a new teacher has discovered, children have no real idea of age.

A first grader in Pittsburgh asked his 22-year-old teacher, "How old are you?"

"How old do you think I am?" she countered.

"Sixty!" he shouted.

Practically in shock, she yelled, "No!" and he asked, "More or less?"

Perhaps the ultimate put-down came in a Franklin, Ohio history class in a discussion of the Civil War. Telling the pupils of the terrible destruction wrought in the South by General Sherman's army, the teacher was interrupted by an earnest question: "Where did you hide?"

Since children say what they think in an unabashed and straightforward way, nothing means more to a teacher than a child's compliment. So you can imagine the warm glow Mrs. Hudson felt when a second grade girl slipped her hand shyly into hers on the playground and said, "Mrs. Hudson, do you know who is the prettiest teacher in the school?"

"No," she replied archly. "Who is?"

"Miss Wilson," she replied.

A teacher who also happens to be a professional pianist was performing for a first grade class, embellishing the song with elaborate runs and extra effects. As she finished a boy said, "Our teacher can play better than you. She can play with *one* hand."

A teacher in Van Nuys, California felt a happy flutter from a child's note that said, "You are my very favorite teacher of all the teachers in the world. You are the prettiest, sweetest and smartest. Thank you for being the most wonderful teacher there ever was."

She was so pleased with the letter that she hardly noticed it was a carbon copy — on the day before report cards came out.

Asking her third graders to do stories, a

teacher gave this example: "Suppose my wish was to be a princess? Then I might write something like this: I have always wanted to be a princess because I would like to live in a castle. I would like to wear long dresses and be very beautiful . . ."

A voice from the back of the room said, "You'll never make it!"

A little boy in Oak Lawn, Illinois came up to his teacher with a big friendly smile and asked, "Do you know why I like you so much?" "No," said the flattered

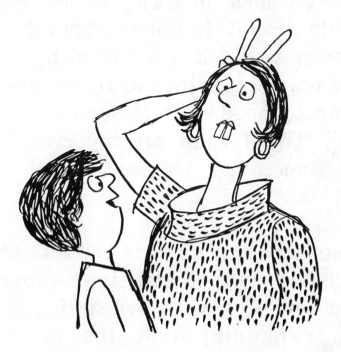

teacher. "Because you have those two big white teeth — just like Bugs Bunny!"

An Evanston, Illinois teacher who confesses to being on the hefty side remembers wearing a new red and white checked dress to school. One polite little boy immediately gave her a compliment: "Your new dress is pretty. You look just like a brick building."

As all teachers know, those little staring eyes are on them all day long, noting the slightest change in their clothes, hair or looks in general. Nothing escapes them, as a teacher who'd had a late night learned while teaching colors to five-year-olds. Trying to prod a child's memory, she asked, "What color are my eyes?" The child glanced up and said, "Red, white and blue."

Another teacher in West Allis, Wisconsin was discussing nonverbal communication with her sixth graders. After explaining that the body can communicate messages through movement

and position, she put her hands on her
waist and tapped her foot, trying to
indicate impatience. Then she asked the
class what she was communicating, and a

boy answered, "You're just trying to look sexy."

You never know what is really going on in a child's mind. First grader Robin kept staring at the teacher's white coral necklace and finally ventured, "Is that all your own teeth in there?"

And eight-year-old Kenny approached a teacher who was wearing a new fur coat. Stroking it, he asked, "Did this used to be somebody's dog?"

In Westfield, Indiana, a girl showed her Thanksgiving sketch to her teacher and asked, "Do you think that Indian looks pregnant?" As the teacher examined the drawing, the girl said, " 'Hmmm,' the Pilgrim's saying, 'you'd better not be.' " A few days later, the girl's mother showed up in a maternity outfit.

Just three months after her marriage, a first-grade teacher showed up at school in a maternity outfit and confided to a friend, "Jim and I weren't planning on a baby this soon. I just don't know how it happened."

A little girl who had been eavesdropping shook her head in disappointment and said, "I thought teachers knew everything."

An Albuquerque, New Mexico teacher came in wearing a blouse that billowed out behind her. A first grade girl eyed her carefully and then asked, "Is that a dress for when you have a baby in the back?"

Sometimes kids get so curious about your personal life that they want to know why, even if you're *not* pregnant. Being asked that question in a southwestern town where small families were rare, a teacher told her class, "I've asked God for children, but so far I've had none."

Juanito, the oldest of eight little Gomezes, replied, "You'd be smart, Miss, to also ask this thing of your husband."

Another teacher in Durellen, New Jersey was startled when a boy slipped behind her, yanked her hair and then ran to his seat. "Was that a nice thing to do?" she asked reproachfully. "No," he admitted,

"But my mom wondered if you wear a wig. Now I can tell her no."

A favorite story of mine comes from Donna Kloker of Great Falls, Montana. One of her junior high students, Larry, shined shoes in a barber shop and wanted her to meet one of the barbers. The boy even gave the barber her phone number — but she had other plans the night he called. A few weeks later, as Donna took her class on a field trip to police court, who should Larry point out but Dave, the barber, paying a traffic ticket. "That's him! That's him!" the boy shouted, and then told Dave, "That's her!" Donna made an excuse to stop at the barber shop a few weeks later, pretending she wanted to see her pupil. She was formally introduced to Dave, and as you've surely guessed by now, Donna and Dave took a shine to each other and got married.

The end of the school year is usually a time of celebration for the teacher as well as her pupils, who often come bearing gifts and hand-made cards to show their affection. One teacher remembers the time her third graders surprised her with a party. As she was opening her gift, a boy scooted by the desk and stage-whispered to the others, "Hey, kids . . . How about the C-A-R-D?"

In Elwood, New Jersey, a teacher was pleased to get a hand-made birthday card from a boy who'd been a lot of trouble all year. On the inside was drawn a birthday cake with these words: "To my beast teacher."

After finishing a student teaching assignment, a young woman in Jericho, New York received several endearing farewell notes from her charges, including one she'll never forget from a boy named Eddie:

"Dear Miss Johnson,
"Sorry you are living."

A boy who had spent two years in the same class in Bellville, Ohio brought his teacher an unintentionally appropriate present — a bottle of perfume called, "Forever Yours."

On the last day of kindergarten, a girl gave her teacher a present, saying, "This is because you're going to miss me."

A woman in Port Jervis, New York will never forget the fourth grade student who usually brought her wine or whiskey at Christmastime because his dad owned a liquor store. One year, the day before Christmas vacation, the boy walked in smiling and placed a box on her desk. Noticing that the box was damp, and assuming he'd dropped it, she touched the bottom with her finger. "Scotch?" she asked. "No," he said, "a puppy."

No one gets stared at more than a teacher who fills in for a day or two. While substituting for a red-haired music teacher, a young woman in West Dundee,

Illinois realized that a first grade girl had been watching her every move all week. Finally the little girl couldn't stand the

suspense any longer and asked, "What did you do with Mrs. Paul's red hair?"

A French teacher in New York was subbing one day in a high school class when a student walked in and asked, "Are you the refill?"

A Los Angeles woman was called to fill in for a first grade teacher. As she walked across the school yard, a small boy confronted her and asked, "Are you going to be our prostitute today?"

Children are always observing, thinking and trying to put it all together. A teacher in El Paso remembers the agile mind of Marty, a freckle-faced seven-year-old who had a new baby brother. In the middle of a reading lesson, the boy pointed to his classmate Nancy, who was wearing a very full skirt, and asked, "Is she pregnant?"

"No," the teacher said. "Lots of little girls wear dresses like that."

The boy glanced around the room again and said, "Are you sure?"

"I'm positive, Marty," she replied. "Now let's finish our lesson."

At that very moment, the girl's mother appeared in the doorway and said, "I've come to pick up Nancy for a doctor's appointment."

The boy gave the teacher one more look as if to say she should have known better.

Every good teacher has something built in that is better than radar. I'd call it a coper. She uses it to cope with kids who would otherwise drive her bananas. A teacher in South Gate, California remembers feeling like going up the wall because a bright, imaginative seven-year-old named Tony had created an invisible companion named Floyd. Having Floyd around wasn't the real problem; it was having to listen to Tony chattering away to his friend all week long. Finally the teacher activated her coper and took action. "I'm tired of your visiting with Floyd in this class," she said. "So I'm going to pick Floyd up and swing him around and throw him out!"

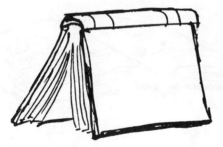

As her arms circled in mid-air, supposedly giving the invisible nuisance the old heave-ho, the next-door teacher walked in and gave her a very odd look. Embarrassed, Tony's teacher turned to him pleadingly and said, "Will you please explain what I'm doing to Floyd?" The boy just smiled and said, "I don't see anything. Floyd's gone home to watch TV."

If there is one quality a teacher needs in abundance, it is patience. A St. Louis, Missouri teacher found hers tested the hard way as she began to explain an examination to her class. A girl interrupted, waving her hand frantically. "I don't have a pencil," she said. "It got stuck in the sharpener." Teacher gave her another, started her instructions again — and got to the same point as the hand went up again. "I tried to write my name," said the girl, "but the pencil is still stuck in the sharpener." The teacher gave her another, started again — and was interrupted once more. *"This* pencil has no eraser. What if I make a mistake?" Groaning, the teacher made sure the third pencil was perfect, and began her

instructions a fourth time. Again the hand popped up, and teacher felt her sanity cracking as she shrieked, "What now?" The girl said, "Would you like to buy some Girl Scout Cookies?"

Kindergarten teachers who work in colder climates soon wish they had majored in advanced snowsuits and galoshes. Zipping and buttoning all those squirmy little kids into winter clothes demands the skill and endurance of a professional wrestler. A Canadian teacher remembers the first snowy day of winter, when her kindergarteners trudged in wearing their new snowsuits. At recess time, a boy asked her help with a suit that had so many buttons, zippers and laces that she had to stretch him out on the floor to get him into it. At last it was on. He looked up and said, "This isn't *my* snowsuit." With all the patience she could muster, she laid him down again, undid the suit, took off his boots — and the boy said, "This suit's my sister's, but my mom said I could wear it today."

Teachers like to meet parents because it helps them round out the family picture of a child, but not all parent-teacher meetings fit the ideal mold. In Binghamton, New York, a junior high teacher in her first year noticed a mother peeking into the room. The teacher introduced herself, but the mother shook her head and said,

"You couldn't be her." "Why?" she asked. The mother said, "I was expecting someone so much older. I mean, well, you're not an 'old witch.' "

During an open house at a school in Modesto, California, a third grader took his father to his desk and showed him an arithmetic problem he had missed on a test. "Can you show me how to do this, Dad?" he asked. The father said, "Why don't you ask your teacher to explain it?" The boy replied, "I don't want to know *that* much."

Show and Tell and Tell and Tell

With all respect to Walter Cronkite and John Chancellor, the nightly network news is no match for the startling and often shocking bulletins blurted out by school kids at Show and Tell Time. A teacher never knows when the usual routine stories about new pets or vacations will be interrupted by a news flash about the private lives of Mom and Dad.

What parents seldom realize or tend to forget is that every little child is a walking recording device, a human tape recorder that can hardly wait until class to play back the family's innermost secrets. Unlike us grown-ups, children have no erase buttons to bleep out highly personal matters. You may think you are having a private conversation in the safety of your own home, but if a small child is within earshot, you may end up as Show and Tell's next headline.

For example, in Denver a girl got up and announced, "My sister is getting married Sunday."

"How wonderful," said the teacher.

"Yes," nodded the girl, "and we hope the baby is a girl."

In Fort Wayne, Indiana, a boy said his family had taken its last trip to Florida,

explaining, "Every time we go down there, mom gets pregnant, so dad says we can't ever go back."

A four-year-old girl proudly told the class how she helps her mother: "I bring her her nightgown in the mornings."

A boy in Flushing, New York announced "My father just had a hook attached to my mother's car."
"Why?" asked teacher.

"Because my mother has an accident almost every week," said the boy, "and he wants to make it easy to tow her away."

Another surprise awaited a Los Angeles teacher when six-year-old Robert ran excitedly into class and said, "Boy, do I have something for Show and Tell this morning." She told him to wait — and wait he did, fidgeting constantly until nine o'clock came. "Okay, Robert," the teacher said, "You've been very patient. It's your turn." The boy pulled up his T-shirt and said, "Look at all my funny little bumps." Yes, it was chicken pox.

After listening to another girl boast about all the presents her daddy brought her, a child in Covina, California told the class, "I don't have a daddy. None of us

kids have a daddy. My mother just had to get her children the best way she could."

A kindergartener in Omaha could hardly wait to tell what happened at a family reunion: "Last Sunday we had this big family party, and my grandma drank so much beer that she fainted."

A boy in North Platte, Nebraska whose parents were separated told why he was so sleepy on Monday mornings. "Daddy comes to see Mommie every Sunday and they giggle all night and I can't sleep."

Discussing the lack of progress of her daughter in kindergarten, a Brooklyn mother told the teacher, "I know she's

not very bright. It takes her a long time to catch on, but I figure that some day at least she could be a kindergarten teacher."

In a rural California area, a mother wrote, "Please excuse Charles for being

late this morning. We had to wait for the hen to lay an egg for his breakfast."

A mother stomped angrily into the

principal's office in Kent, Washington, and complained about a teacher, saying, "My daughter can't understand the directions, examples or anything else that $¢%& teacher says. My girl just has no contraceptive of what she's talking about."

Fortunately, not all parents show up to complain. Occasionally a parent has a kind word for the hard-working teacher. In Thiells, New York, a teacher got a note saying that one of her second graders had enjoyed his class. "Thank you so much," said mother, "for creating an atmosphere that *simulates* learning."

Notes from home often enliven a teacher's day, like this one from a mother in Sepulveda, California: "Please excuse Jon for being absent from school this morning, as he went to the hospital to help me bring his new baby sister home. Please be assured it will not happen again this term."

In Grand Rapids, Michigan, a teacher

received this note: "Please excuse Jim for being absent yesterday. I kept him home as a preventive so his cough wouldn't get worse. Now I'm in bed recovering from trying to keep him in bed yesterday."

The same teacher also received this note: "Joey was absent because he has had a cold. But his fever is gone and he feels better, so you've got him back. Thank God for teachers!"

Hang Him on a Hook
in the Coatroom

Some teachers have a marvelous gift for keeping a class orderly and attentive. When they walk in, like a star making an entrance on Broadway, an expectant hush descends over the room. Their mere presence seems to create a "learning situation," which is officialese for a class where everybody quiets down long enough to absorb the lesson.

But most teachers have to work hard for discipline. It can be an all-day struggle that calls for the patience of a saint, the heart of a lion tamer and the endurance of a hockey player. Depending on the class ratio of angels to hellions, a good day can be any day that the teacher survives without being led away to a rest home.

I'll admit right now that I could never

be a teacher. I did try teaching — in Sunday School — and I loved working with kids. But it was all I could do to keep those youngsters in hand, let alone teach them anything. As any parent knows, keeping *one* rambunctious kid in line can be a full-time job. Multiply that situation by thirty or so, and you have a rough idea of what a classroom can be like.

Looking back on my own school days, I was what people call "a good boy." I was even good in high school. My grades dropped when I started going out with girls, but I never got into any trouble. I do remember being disciplined once — in kindergarten. I giggled during nap time, so the teacher made me go sit behind the piano. I spent a long time living that down.

One disciplinary chore that teachers inherit is yard duty, the patrolling of the school grounds during recess or lunch to see that everyone behaves — or comes as close as they can. A teacher in Hollywood tells of being on yard duty recently when a little girl ran up, all out of breatn, and said, "Two boys are fighting near the lunch benches, and I think the one on the bottom wants to see you."

In Virginia Beach, Virginia a teacher had endured all she could take of her chatterbox first graders, so she told them, "I'm tired! Tired of asking you to be quiet, tired of telling you to be quiet, tired of trying to make you listen — and tired of the noise. What should I do?"

A boy raised his hand in the silence that followed and made a suggestion: "Why don't you take a nap?"

In Greeley, Colorado, a teacher gritted her teeth as one kid after another slammed the classroom door. Finally she blew her stack: "The next one to do that gets spanked on a bare bottom," she said. Moments later the door slammed again with a terrific bang and in walked the principal.

A teacher in Far Rockaway, New York could feel the tears coming after a painful

encounter with an unruly class. Just then the assistant principal came in and told the students, "This looks like a fine class, but I just received an extremely poor report from your last-period teacher. I want you to understand that I am not here to reprimand you for your conduct, because I know we all have our good days and bad

days. I just want to know who threw the chair out of the window.''

Sometimes teachers turn the other cheek and try to think positively about their troublesome charges. In Taylorsville, North Carolina, Billy was a real monster, and all the kids knew it. One day when he was absent, the teacher seized her chance to change everyone's attitude, and invited the other boys and girls to pick out all the good points Billy had. As they were ready to begin, a boy said, "We're sure gonna have to lie a lot."

In Brooklyn, a teacher sent home a note saying, "The boy is a good student, but he talks too much." The card came back with a father's written comment: "You should meet his mother."

A second grade teacher in Nanuet, New York wrote a note to the parents of a bright but very talkative boy, complaining that he interrupted class every five minutes. The mother replied, "I'm sorry my son has been such a problem to you. At home we take an aspirin."

In the town of California, Maryland, a teacher was warned about a fiery little half-pint redhead who was being put in her class on the first day school resumed. So she went to his previous second grade teacher, a tiny woman, and asked, "What

do I do with him when he misbehaves?" The answer: "I pick him up and hang him on a hook in the coatroom."

Not all notes get as far as the intended

parents, as a teacher in Lansing, Illinois discovered when she sent home a report about the poor behavior of a little boy, saying, "Have your father sign this and bring it back." The next day the boy returned with the note. It was signed, "My father."

Discipline is basically a parent's job, it seems to me, and yet many parents either look to the school to do it, or shirk the job entirely. In Reedsburg, Wisconsin, the principal summoned an eighth grade boy's parents to a conference and explained that their son was a real problem, adding, "You'll just have to let him grow up if he is to amount to anything. Does he have any responsibilities at home at all?"

"Why, yes," replied his mother. "He has to brush his teeth."

Ask a teacher about her most unforgettable student, and it may well be one who was a holy terror. In Olympia, Washington, a teacher recalls a seventh grader named Bill who broke every rule in existence. His specialties in her class were the sneaky but well-aimed spitwad and the tripping foot quicker than the eye.

"Students walking past his desk were suddenly afflicted with the lurches," she says. "I was the only one who ever got past his desk without stumbling a few yards."

One afternoon while the rest of the class read a play, Bill unscrewed his ballpoint pen and snapped the ink stem. The ink went everywhere — his desk, the floor, his papers, his jeans — so the teacher ordered him to come in after school.

Miraculously, the boy showed up. "It was my perfect opportunity to get back at this kid after weeks of torment," the teacher said, being only human. So she had him wash desks, clean blackboards, stack dictionaries and then scrub away on his hands and knees with a janitor's brush. After a long time, the teacher heard him muttering a plea that forever changed him in her mind from demon to human. He said, "Oh, fairy Godmother,

Excuses can become works of art in the minds of imaginative kids. In Carson, California, a boy who was often tardy came in with this explanation for the morning: "You won't believe this, teacher, but the reason I'm late today is beyond my control. A bird flew in and knocked over my alarm clock."

A Seattle boy who was usually quite conscientious about his homework showed up one day without his math paper. "Why didn't you do your math?" the teacher asked.

"I did," the boy said. "I had it all finished — and then my little brother ate it."

Another dawdler wandered into class fifteen minutes late in Oakland, California, carrying a rather large tortoise.

"Sorry I'm late," he said, "but I couldn't help it. My turtle followed me to school."

A shop class teacher in Montrose, California had an idea for dealing with two boys who were chronically late to class. Since it was World Series time and both boys were avid ballplayers, he told them they should pretend the next day that they were trying to leg out an inside-the-park home run. Two minutes before the tardy bell, the first boy came running in, all smiles, and sat down. With

thirty seconds to go, the class could hear footsteps pounding closer, and everybody began yelling, "Faster!" The second boy zoomed into the doorway at top speed, sliding on his backside right into the teacher's desk as his buddy stood up and yelled, "Safe!"

A teacher in Phoenix remembers one of her tougher boys who brought her a rose every day for several weeks. But one morning he came without it, so she asked, "Didn't you forget something?" "I'm sorry about your rose," he said. "The lady was looking and I couldn't swipe one."

Sometimes, despite all that teachers can do, it's the students who have the last word. In Brooklyn, a teacher remembers being in charge of the high school auditorium which was being used as a detention center for the boys and girls who had been unruly that day. Suddenly from the back of the room came a shrill voice saying, "Give me liberty or give me death."

Being onstage, the teacher couldn't see who had cried out, so when the laughter died down, he yelled, "Who said that?" "Patrick Henry," came the answer.

But surely one of the most harrowing experiences a teacher has ever undergone happened in another Brooklyn school, on the fourth floor of a tall building. The room had a balcony that could not be seen

by the day's substitute teacher, a young woman. When she reprimanded one of the junior high students for making trouble in class, warning she would send him to the dean, the boy shouted: "Okay! You asked for it. I'm going to kill myself."

With that he ran to the open window beside the balcony and dived through. The teacher stared for an instant at the disappearing body which was apparently hurtling to death four flights below, and collapsed in a faint!

A teacher earning extra money as a summer camp counselor was utterly exhausted by supervising dozens of yelling and screaming kids all day. One of her biggest headaches was a rather spoiled youngster who kept running up to her, insisting that she think of some new game he could play. Her nerves finally snapped when he came back for the umpteenth time and asked, "What do you want me to play now?" Muttering to herself between clenched teeth, she said, "Russian roulette."

A Peanut Butter Heart

When I was five years old, my mother would give me a nickel for the streetcar and I would ride clear across town, all by myself, to kindergarten. In those days, a trip like that was considered perfectly safe for a child.

We kids spent our days listening to nursery stories, learning to draw with crayons and sometimes making fun things like valentines. I remember giving my first valentine to little Patty Darrough, a beautiful blue-eyed blonde. I was crazy about her. Eventually we went all through school together — but not as sweethearts. I fell in love with my wife Marge in high school, and Patty married a writer on the West Coast.

Since I was a kindergarten veteran by the time I reached the first grade, the teacher gave me a very responsible job — escorting everyone else to the bathroom when they had to go. It really was important, because if I didn't take them, they would run home!

Looking back on my own childhood and comparing it to the life of today's youngsters, I suppose the most significant difference lies in the all-pervasive influence of television. It's incredible to me that the average child spends more time in front of the tube than he does in class, yet the experts say this is true. And the experiences teachers have with the very young seem to bear this out.

A pre-schooler looking at a picture book asked his teacher, "What are those kids doing?" "Playing ring around the rosy," he was told. "Do you know 'ring around the rosy'?" "No," the boy said, "I know 'ring around the collar.'"

In Newington, Connecticut, an honest little soul turned in a lost coin and the gym teacher asked his first graders, "Who lost a dime?" Several hands went up, so

to settle the matter, he said he would give
the dime to the person who could identify
the picture on it. Little Karen was the

winner when she answered, "Walter Cronkite."

In Needham Heights, Massachusetts, a teacher had spent the day telling first graders about the contributions of the Spanish to American culture and language. Reviewing later, she mentioned words like lariat, rodeo and coyote, and asked what language they came from. "I know," said a boy. "You're talking Cowboy."

TV obviously had its impact on a little girl who was asked if her mother was too busy to come to the phone. "She's pretty busy all right," the girl said. "She's watching a book."

Another teacher in Ft. Bragg, North Carolina had a little girl in class who was constantly popping up out of her seat. So when the teacher went to the main office, she had an idea and flipped on the intercom switch to her classroom. "Sit down, Betty," she commanded. The girl, who *was* out of her seat, looked around with an awed expression and sat down quickly, saying, "Yes, Jesus."

Little Bobby's family took him along to see the launching of a ship named after his uncle, a famous war hero. When he returned to school in Indio, California the next day, his kindergarten teacher said, "I saw a picture of you and your family on the news last night. Would you tell the class what you did yesterday?"

Bobby nodded proudly and said, "I went to the Navy shipyard for lunch. My grandmother took a bottle of shampoo and smashed it against the side of the ship. She hit that ship so hard it broke away and went all the way out to the ocean."

Children can be just as logical as any adult, but they have to make do with the few facts they know, often with surprising results. A Canadian teacher in Hamilton, Ontario tells of leaving her kindergarten class playing quietly while she went to the principal's office for a message. While there, she decided to surprise the class by talking to them over the public address system. "Good morning, kindergarten children," she said. "How nicely and quietly you are playing." There was absolute silence after she spoke, because the kids weren't used to the p.a. system. But when she returned to the room, a boy said, "While you were gone, the walls were talking to us!"

A Vineland, New Jersey, teacher thought

her class understood everything about fire drills at the nursery schoolhouse because there were frequent drills to acquaint the children with the large chute that led from the second floor to the ground. But when a new girl saw the chute and asked her playmate what it was, the veteran explained: "Suppose we're playing out here and the house catches on fire. We have to run in the house, run upstairs and come down that chute."

Youngsters may not know the answer to a teacher's question, but quite often they will come up with something plausible that makes a sensible answer to them. In Chelmsford, Massachusetts, a teacher was discussing policemen as community helpers. "Why do you suppose policemen wear white gloves?" the teacher asked. A fashion-conscious little girl replied, "Because white goes with everything."

Down in Titusville, Florida, a fat blimp floated over the schoolyard as the children came running out for recess. "Look!" a girl yelled to her playmate. "That

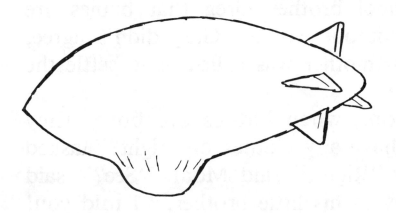

airplane's gonna have a baby!"

In Hartsdale, New York, a first grader named Larry was explaining to his pre-school brother Greg that babies are born without clothes. Greg didn't agree, so their mother was called in to settle the dispute.

"Mom, when babies are born, they don't have any clothes on, right?" asked Larry. "Right," said Mom. "See?" said the boy to his little brother, "I told you! Just a blanket."

Teachers often use Aesop's Fables and similar stories to teach a moral on behavior to children. But what the teacher intends to show by her story and what kids get out of it are often two different things, as a Brooklyn teacher discovered when she read the class the fable about the fox who flattered the crow so it would start singing — and drop a piece of cheese from its mouth that the fox wished to eat.

"What does that story teach us?" she asked, seeking the moral about flattery. There was a long silence, and finally a boy volunteered: "It teaches us never to talk with our mouths full."

A class in Glendale, California studied

the story of "The Blind Men and the Elephant," in which each blind man, after feeling part of the animal, has a different idea of what the elephant appears to be. "What do we learn from this story?" the teacher asked, and a boy replied, "What you feel ain't what you get."

In Bowling Green, Kentucky, a class read "The Emperor's New Clothes," and the teacher brought out the idea that the emperor thought he had clothes on, but really didn't. She asked, "What is it the Emperor is doing?" and a girl said, "I think he's streaking."

A third grader in North Hollywood, California caught his teacher by surprise after a reading of "Cinderella" by saying, "How come Cinderella's clothes turned back into rags, but her shoes stayed the same?" While teacher was still puzzling that one out, a bright little girl came up with an answer: "Because they were made out of stuff that wasn't bio-degradable."

Another logical nursery school

youngster listened to the rhyme about
Humpty Dumpty and said, "If all those
guys were there, why didn't they just catch
him?"

Another fantasy character who seems to
be known to every little American boy and
girl is the Tooth Fairy. In Melrose,

Massachusetts, a girl returned to class to tell of having the dentist pull a tooth that morning. A classmate asked, "Do you think the Tooth Fairy pays extra when a dentist pulls your tooth?" "I don't even have it," said the girl. "The dentist keeps all the teeth he pulls. That's how he makes his money."

A Brooklyn girl asked, "Will the Tooth Fairy give everybody a dime whose teeth

are out?" Told that the fairy would, the girl said, "My granddaddy ought to have a lot of dimes."

Every classroom is a gathering of little poets, philosophers, doers and dreamers. Some kids have imaginations that soar away at the slightest touch, like kites on a summer's day. Others are more down-to-earth, best at logical problem-solving like the practical grown-ups they will be.

The language of poetry comes easily to a child's lips. A girl arrives at school clutching a wilted rose and presents it to her teacher, saying, "It was pretty when I picked it, but now it's fainted." Another girl taking a walk with her class exclaims, "Oh look! Our line is all wrinkled."

One of my favorite poets is the first grader in Ellisville, Missouri whose teacher noticed he wasn't his usual energetic self. "Don't you feel well?" she asked. "No," he said, "I think I've got peanut butter stuck to my heart."

A teacher in Hobart, Indiana had spent

a long hard day trying to persuade a seven-year-old to do his classwork. Sitting down to write a report to his parents, she didn't realize how thin her patience had worn until the boy read the note and said, "Boy! You even yelled on my paper!"

Some children are born philosophers. When a Brooklyn teacher asked her first graders if they knew anything about Mother's Day, a boy replied, "This is the day on which we forgive our mothers for what they do to us the rest of the year."

Another glimpse into a child's notion of others is afforded by the girl in Skokie, Illinois who defined a sweater as "something I have to put on when my mother is cold."

In Annville, Pennsylvania, a teacher tried to combine a lesson on directions with the chore of handing in homework, asking the children to pass their papers to the east. After the uproar that followed, the teacher showed them a compass that indicated the east was to the right. The next time she tried it, there was more pandemonium, but one boy in the middle of the room remained calm and simply raised his hand to ask, "Teacher, why do you punish yourself like this?"

A grammar school principal in Levelland, Texas fell victim to his own daughter's logic when she asked her mother

why daddy stayed late at school so much. The mother explained that daddy couldn't always get his work done during school hours, so the girl asked, "Why don't they put daddy in a slower group?"

Children are naturally limited in their background for problem-solving, but if you give them a problem within their own experience, they can often do as well or better than any adult. An elementary school secretary in Augusta, Georgia found this out when she went to the classroom for the coat of a boy who was in the nurse's room, ill and waiting to go home. The problem was that no one, including the teacher, knew which coat was the boy's. Another boy suggested, "Let's all go to the back of the room and put our coats on, and the one that's left will be his." They tried it, and sure enough, it worked.

Synonym Toast

A good teacher will change your life. She makes your classroom and your world come alive, and you with it. And while you are learning the pleasures of learning, she is busy studying, too. She is studying *you* . . . to encourage the best that is in you. In fact, that is what "education" literally means — to bring out what lies within.

My bringer-outer and life-changer was Mary Miller, our high school English teacher back home in Danville, Illinois. Her students were her whole existence. She was into everything that involved us: she knew who was going steady with whom, who'd had a fight and who'd made up. Everything we did or cared about she cared about.

If it hadn't been for Mary Miller, I might

be on an unemployment line today. She's the one who got after me to perform in the Dramatic Club and, thanks to her encouragement, I had the lead in practically every play in school.

Miss Miller made us work, really work, but her classes had a way of being fun. She opened us up by having us memorize passages from literature and then do them in front of the class. When the term ended, we could talk about or demonstrate whatever topic we wanted to. I remember that I was very big on magic in those days, so I devised a show and tell on how magicians use misdirection to obtain their marvelous effects. She gave me an A-plus for my sleight-of-hand; but as I look back, I realize she was doing magic in that classroom all year long.

Even though Mrs. Miller's English class was my favorite, I can't say I enjoyed studying the rules of grammar. So I can sympathize with the little boy who was having trouble writing about his summer vacation, and said, "It is a puzzle about swim, swam and swum. Swim is what I

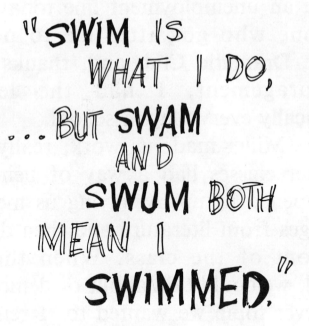

do, but swam and swum both mean I swimmed."

Much of the unintentional humor in children's talk comes from half-heard words that they think they know and then try to use, with totally unexpected results. In Dorchester, Massachusetts, for example, a class had struggled to master the difficult *fl* sound in *flag*. The next new word was *flute,* and a boy said he knew that one. Raising his right hand to his heart, he explained, "Every day we flute the flag."

Sometimes that slightly tangled way of speaking persists into adult life. Bandleader Bob Crosby used to tell stories about a drummer of his who was a chronic malapropper and word scrambler. Coming back from a winter vacation, the drummer reported that he had had a lot of fun on a "tobobbin," but that it had been so cold he had to wear "ear muffins."

That drummer has a rival growing up in Albany, New York, where his art teacher heard him tell another boy, "Stop criminizing me." The other boy smiled and said, "It's criticize." Disgusted, the first boy said, "What do you think you are? A puefessor?"

Working on consonant blends, a Larned, Kansas teacher asked her second graders for a word using "Br," and got the right answer, "Broth." "Oh, I know what that is," a classmate said. "My mother has a stretch broth."

At a parochial school in Norfolk, Virginia, the class learned that they would always find the blend *tr* in the word *trouble.* A few days later, as they studied the sacraments, a boy said, "Look! There's *trouble,* right in the middle of *matrimony.*"

Most grown-ups will avoid using a word unless they are fairly sure of what it means, but kids are far less inhibited. If they have any inkling of a word's meaning, they'll toss it right at you.

A teacher in the Bronx was teaching the poem "Sea Lullaby" to his class, and asked if anyone knew what a lullaby was. A boy replied, "That's when the police try to come and arrest you and you say, 'You can't do that, because I have a lullaby.'"

A teacher in Ferdinand, Indiana asked if anyone knew what "literature" is. Only one child raised her hand, and she said, "It's like when a cat has kittens."

Some fourth graders were stumped on the word "mature" in their Colorado Springs class until a youngster said, "That's what smells when you put it on your lawn."

Some teachers will go to almost any lengths to dramatize a point for a child, like the Norwich, Connecticut man who was trying to get little Richard to pronounce the "j" sound in "giant." Finally the instructor took off his shoes and stood on Richard's reading table, towering over the group. "You're all little people," he said, "and I'm a great big . . . "J-E-R-K!" shouted Richard.

A teacher in Sterling Heights, Michigan tells of spending several lessons on when to use the words *saw, seen* and *have seen*. Reviewing one last time to see if the class understood why "I seen it" is incorrect, she gave up after a boy explained, "I use

... AND I'M A GREAT BIG ...

J-E-R-K!

see when I'm looking at it now, and the word *saw* when I seen it."

A New York class of fifth graders was reviewing base words and how they change in form and meaning. "Think of as many words as possible related to the base word 'delegate,' " teacher said. The children responded with "delegation," "delegating," and "delegated." Then a

Brooklyn girl suggested one more . . .
"delegatessen."

Finishing a lesson on the use of possessives, the teacher asked:

"What is the possessive form of boy?"

Answer: "Girl."

After explaining about opposites — such as in-out, up-down — the instructor asked for the opposite of "right" — and a black student confidently answered "on!"

One subject I always found easy in school was spelling. I just had a natural feeling for it, and used to win a lot of spelldowns. Remember those days? The teacher would give you a word, and you'd have to sit down if you missed it. The last one left standing became the champ. I still remember the word that set me down more than once . . . diphtheria. (Or is it D-I-P-T-H-A-R-I-A?)

A Reseda, California teacher tells of asking a boy to name the spelling book he had used the previous semester. "It was called *Success in Spelling*," the boy answered. "Will you write that down for me," asked the teacher, "so I can remember the one you used?" "Sure," said the boy, "but how do you spell success?"

A seven-year-old in Crown Point, Indiana was writing about the news in her life, and asked how to spell "knees." Pointing to the girl's knees to make sure that was what she meant, the teacher told her . . . and the girl wrote, "The brown knees are having a Halloween party."

Returning home after a spelling test, a boy confessed he got the word "please" wrong in a spelling test . . . but he knew why, explaining: "I hardly ever use it."

Another creative speller surprised his teacher when he wrote, "Most of New York City's water supply comes from two great dames upstate."

Reading and grading compositions for long hours after school is a grind, but occasionally a blooper surfaces that makes it all worthwhile. A Los Angeles teacher tells of a seventh grader's book report:

"It had been several years since Jim had seen Sally. Not since they were sweethearts in high school. After Jim finished college, he renude his friendship with her."

Introducing new vocabulary words, a Seattle teacher asked if any of her third graders knew the word "dusk." A boy replied, "That's the stuff that grows on furniture."

Ninth graders in Los Angeles were given a vocabulary test, and one ingenious child defined "prowess" as "a lady prowler."

Even when a teacher explains a new word, she can't always be sure that her class got the message. A Chicago teacher learned this one day when she explained that calling a soil fertile means it is very rich. A boy nodded happily in seeming understanding and said, "I want to be fertile when I grow up."

Here are some more word "experts":

In Evanston, Illinois, a girl defined a honeymoon as "the time when the marriage is consumed."

And a classmate of hers thought that graffiti were "what people throw at you at parades."

In a Bronx class where most of the youngsters speak Spanish, the teacher told the youngsters to write a summary of a story they had just read. A girl raised her hand to ask what a summary is, and a classmate answered confidently, "A summary is a boat that goes underwater."

In Roselle Park, New Jersey, a teacher asked if anyone knew the word "synonym." A boy answered, "That's what I had on my toast this morning."

A Philadelphia class was starting a class discussion on reflections, but no one seemed to know the word until a boy volunteered, "A reflection is when somebody hits you in the knee real hard and your leg kicks.''

In Council Bluffs, Iowa, a class being given a test on sports terms was asked to define ''tackle.'' The teacher's favorite answer was that of a girl who wrote, ''Tackle is the past tense of tickle.''

Sometimes a child's definition is far superior to the one you'll find in the dictionary. A girl in Lauderdale Lakes, Florida came up with an imaginative picture when she defined a ''rash'' as ''when your skin feels like it's wearing a rug.''

After discussing the Nile region and its early civilization, an instructor in Pasadena, California asked the class, ''Does anyone know what a fez is?''
''Sure,'' said a boy. ''The Egyptian police.''

Quite often the way a child uses a word will reveal his mind hard at work, even if he's wrong. A youngster in Forest Hills,

New York had obviously read about ancient creatures like the brontosaurus when he defined a "thesaurus" as "the offspring of a prehistoric animal."

Another boy in Lancaster, Pennsylvania thought he knew what a "florist" was — "A man who puts carpets on your floors."

A kindergartener in Paramount, California complained to her mother that the teacher sent the class out to recess, but nobody knew how to recess — so they just played instead.

The need to master new words in school sometimes continues long after the primary grades. One English teacher was telling a high school class how important it is to have a vast, readily usable speaking vocabulary. "If you make use of the same word at least ten times," he said, "you can claim it forever." At that moment a petite blonde in the rear of the classroom could be heard murmuring, "Jim . . . Jim . . . Jim . . ."

Once a teacher turns on a child's imagination, it often keeps running all by itself. In Brooklyn, some second graders had just read the story of a woodchopper and his family, and teacher decided to have them dramatize it. A boy asked, "Can I play the tree?" "Go ahead," said the teacher, wondering how he'd do it. As

the woodsman swung his imaginary axe at
the "tree," the boy said, "Mmmmm!
That smarts," and backed away. "Why
did you back up?" asked the teacher, and
the "tree" said, "I saw a dog coming."

In Orlando, Florida, a reading group was presenting a play about a couple getting married. As the "bride" and "groom" came down the aisle, another boy showered them with handfuls of tiny bits of paper. Noticing the teacher's disapproving look, the boy said, "I was throwing rice . . . but don't worry, it'll be cleaned up in a second. It was minute rice."

It was Halloween time, and a teacher in Lake Charles, Louisiana had readied an impromptu play for her fourth graders. A ghost, a monster, a witch and a bat were in the first scene, and the bat's only line was "Eek, eek!" Teacher chose a shy, withdrawn girl to play the bat, thinking the tiny part would be psychologically right to help her come out of her shell.

But when the bat's big moment came, teacher heard four sounds in rapid succession: 1 — "Eek, eek!" 2 — A bat running toward the stage door. 3 — A door slamming. 4 — Another little actor explaining, "The bat wet the floor."

Frequently when they don't know all the facts they need, kids fill in the gaps with imaginative ideas that *seem* quite logical. A class in Des Moines was talking about Indian costumes when the teacher pointed to a picture and asked, "Why do you suppose the Indians wear bells around their ankles?" A boy answered thoughtfully, "So the cowboys can hear them coming."

In Cinnaminson, New Jersey, children were waiting anxiously to perform in the annual spring concert for parents. A teacher turned to one of her first graders and asked, "Are you nervous?" "No," said the boy, "just my knees are."

Although he created our finest literature, Shakespeare never made it to high school; at least, not *my* high school. Now, I love to hear his words performed, because there's so much music to them, but

unlike so many actors I've never really had the urge to play Hamlet. While we didn't have the bard back in Danville, we did have literary heroes like Mark Twain, Edgar Allen Poe and Booth Tarkington. I loved everything Twain and Poe ever wrote, but my favorite character was

Tarkington's "Penrod," with whom I identified because he was a typical midwestern kid, just like me and my buddies.

Today there is no doubt whether Shakespeare is to be or not to be taught. But what is learned . . . that is the question we might ask when we read students' efforts like these:

"Cassius was a stinker all the way through the play. He reeked havoc because of his jealousy."

"Polonius is a very stupid person. This is shown by his lack of intelligence."

"In Hamlet, Claudius kills his brother and commits incest because he is ambitious to attain his brother's place. Other than this he does not appear to have committed any serious crime."

Here are a few more literary comments from free-wheeling essay writers:

"Hester Prynne was made to wear the

scarlet letter. It stood for the sin she had committed — adultercourse."

"Willy Loman's suicide was the fulfillment of his dreams and ambitions."

After reading a medieval ballad on the Virgin Mary, a parochial schoolgirl wrote: "The theme of this poem is that behind every successful man there is a woman."

A future political scientist writing a paper on current events had warning for us all:

"The reason we shouldn't H-bomb Russia is because if we were to drop a bomb on Russia they would probably drop one on us and this would go on and on and finally lead to war."

If that kind of logic makes you shake your head consider the third grader who was doing a composition on why trees are so important to us, and wrote: "If we didn't have trees, firemen wouldn't have anything to climb up to rescue cats that were stuck in them."

Budding writers are often advised to express themselves with force, brevity and complete honesty. It would be hard to surpass the fourth grade girl who wrote a two-word composition on what she liked about school: "Nothing much."

The Nina, the Pinta
and the Toyota

All I remember about history is having to memorize an apparently endless number of irrelevant dates and places. Maybe I never really learned them as well as I should have because we kids took advantage of our teacher, who was elderly and quite hard of hearing. It was something of a game to answer a question of hers, like "When did Columbus discover America?" with "1776" . . . and see her nod her head in satisfaction because she thought you had said "1492."

I must confess a twinge of guilt whenever I'm tempted to say that I didn't like a subject because such-and-such a teacher didn't inspire me. I know now that much more would have been available to me in school if I had worked harder and done my own part. Fortunately, most subjects came easily to me. My grades were always quite good, until I reached high school and switched my major to girls.

Today I have a thought somewhere in

GIDDY UP

the back of my mind to return to school. I would love to go to a college or university full time, possibly even earning that degree

I never had. Who knows? I might even enjoy history, this time around, if *I* can hear the teacher.

Although I never liked cramming dates and battles into my head, I did enjoy stories of American heroes like George Washington. There must have been a whole classful of kids like me in Brooklyn on the day a teacher was explaining about the equestrian statue of Washington near their school. The year 1777, as he reminded them, will always be remembered for a critical winter's encampment in Pennsylvania. In dramatic tones, he pictured the starved Continental soldiers huddled about their fires as General Washington made his rounds, urging his weary mount through the deep snows. Finally, to make sure they would always remember Valley Forge, the teacher asked a visibly moved class: "What two words are carved for all time into the base of the statue?" After a deep silence came a questioning answer: "Giddy Up?"

A kindergarten teacher in an apartment house section of Hollywood recalls showing his class a picture of Mount Vernon, explaining, "This is where George Washington lived." The children stared at the building for several moments until one finally asked, "Which floor?"

Another class in Woodbridge, New Jersey was studying a portrait of Washington when the teacher happened to mention that George had a set of wooden false teeth. "No *wonder* he isn't smiling," exclaimed a girl.

During the patriotic month of February, a class had been learning about the Flag and its various names . . . Old Glory, the Star Spangled Banner, and the Stars and Stripes. After telling the legendary story of Betsy Ross and George Washington, the teacher reviewed the lesson and asked:
"Who can tell me who Washington went to see about making a Flag?"
A boy in the front row answered: "Old Gloria."

The Weekly Reader showed a picture of the *Mayflower,* so a teacher in Edwards,

New York asked her first graders if they knew anything about it. "Oh, sure," said a boy. "That was the ship George

Washington sailed on when he discovered America.''

Another group of first graders down in New Orleans studied a reader with a silhouette of the sixteenth President of the United States. ''What is this man's name?'' the teacher asked. A boy answered, ''I know all about *him*. His name is President Birmingham Lincoln and he was a free slave.''

Stressing Lincoln's greatness, a kindergarten teacher in Los Angeles told her pupils, ''We still remember Mr. Lincoln even though he has been dead for over a hundred years.''
''Oh, he's not dead,'' a boy objected. ''He's alive! I saw him at Disneyland.''

Even more impressed with Honest Abe was a girl whose essay declared that Lincoln was ''born in a log cabin which he built with his own hands.''

The whole concept of time is confusing for first and second graders, who often

think that Washington and Lincoln were the best of friends. A teacher in Grand Island, New York, was winging it without the textbook one day, and admitted she couldn't remember which President came first — Monroe or Madison. "Gosh," said a surprised boy, "I never even knew Marilyn was President."

After a short group discussion of Lincoln as a child, a teacher in De Witt, New York asked, "What did Abraham Lincoln become when he grew up?" A girl confidently replied, "President Nixon."

The confusion keeps growing as children study the lesser-known modern Presidents. A boy thought that Teddy Roosevelt was the one who "irrigated" the Panama Canal. Another wrote that Woodrow Wilson "opposed secret treaties and strongly favored open convents."

During a discussion of early America, a class of fifth graders in Woodland Hills, California learned that the Pilgrims wore dark clothing with white collars. The teacher explained that dark clothing was practical in those days because it didn't have to be washed so often. Then she asked, "But why did they wear white collars?" A boy who evidently does his homework in front of the television set answered, "So they wouldn't show their dandruff."

A boy in East Rockaway, New York was sure he knew the name of the President who led us out of the Depression: "Franklin D. Roosevelt Drive." (His teacher was tempted to ask him if the Father of our country was the

GEORGE WASHINGTON BRIDGE

ABRAHAM LINCOLN MEMORIAL

FRANKLIN D. ROOSEVELT DRIVE

George Washington Bridge.)

After telling her kindergarteners about the first Thanksgiving, a teacher in Queens, New York asked, "Who remembers the name of the boat that brought the Pilgrims to America?" A boy answered, "The Cauliflower."

During an eighth grade history class in Visalia, California, a student was asked to write a character sketch of Miles Standish. He gave this response: "When it came to war, Miles was a brave and honest man. But when it came to love, he was like a second grader doing eighth grade work."

Another favorite children's character in history is the man who discovered America, known to at least one youngster as "Misterpher Columbus." Another boy in La Porte, Indiana, who is obviously a TV fan, thought the man was "Columbo."

A seven-year-old in Okemos, Michigan balked at the notion that Columbus had shown our planet is round. "I don't believe the earth is round," he said, "because everybody always talks about going to the four corners of it."

The day after hearing about Columbus, a first grader in Garland, Texas ran up to his teacher and said, "I remember the names of his ships . . . the Nina, the Pinta and the Toyota."

On the birthday of a famous composer, the Holy Cross School in Omaha had the custom of piping his music throughout the school at lunchtime. After the children heard the *Hallelujah Chorus* from Handel's *Messiah,* a Sister asked her class to tell whose birthday they were celebrating. A boy yelled, "George Frederic Doorknob!"

Here are a few more slightly off-key observations from music historians of uncertain note:

"My favorite composer is Opus."

"Gregory (of the famous chant) lived from 540 to 604, but I forget whether it was AC or DC."

"My best-loved piece is the Bronze Lullaby."

"Henry Purcell is a well-known composer few people have ever heard of."

Seeking that famous quote about having but one life to give for his country, a history teacher in East Rockaway, New York asked the class:

"What was the last thing Nathan Hale said before being hung as an American spy?"

The answer: "Help!"

During a lesson on William Tell, a teacher in Winston-Salem asked, "What is the difference between being born of gentle birth, and born of peasant birth?"

A girl from a large family volunteered, "One is when you have the doctor, and the other is when you don't."

A seven-year-old in Los Angeles defined the Depression as "a long time ago when instead of people becoming millionaires, millionaires became people."

Nothing lightens a teacher's task at paper-grading time more than an occasional blooper, like these from examinations:

What was the Industrial Revolution?

"It was the change from Reproduction in the home to Reproduction in the factory."

Name two hardships endured by the South during the Civil War.

"The *Monitor* and the *Merrimac*."

Define the term "to bear arms."

"You may wear sleeveless dresses."

What is Democracy?

"Democracy is that system of government where one man is as good as the next, and sometimes a lot better."

"Drake made England a leading sea power by defeating the invisible Spanish Armada."

What was the first permanent settlement made by the Europeans in Florida?

"Miami Beach."

The Incans used what animals for wool?

"Woolves."

Essay writers produced off-center answers like these:

"The blocks of stone used to build the pyramids in ancient Egypt were dragged up the ramp by sheer union labor."

"Greek fighters would wrestle until one conceived."

"During the French Revolution, excessive murders were committed on each person."

"The Russian peasants lived in mud huts with lots of rough mating on the floor."

"The workers all worked very hard, but all the money they made went to fill the coiffures of the wealthy."

"Cyrus McCormick invented the raper and put thousands of men out of work."

"I liked Thomas a Becket best because he loved his people. He was a brilliant and wonderful man. His own dear friends killed him."

Give Me Puberty
or Give Me Death

Geography was always fun for me in school. I loved studying maps and globes, and learning about all the lands and peoples of the world. And now that I have a boat to sail in San Diego, California, I'm back poring over the charts again, having more fun than ever, learning ocean navigation and using what little math I learned.

As a fellow with an acute case of mathophobia in my school days, I can sympathize with the frustrated kids in New York City who had barely struggled through old-fashioned long division when they found out they'd have to start all over with the so-called new math. To make them feel better, the school's math coordinator assured them that new math was easier. But as the class squirmed through the new way, a girl asked, "Can't we do it the hard way? It's easier."

I like the story of the South Gate, California math teacher whose student told her, "I'm having trouble with eagles." She was mystified until he explained, "Like 1 and 1 eagles 2, 2 plus 2 eagles 4."

While going over a complicated homework assignment for her math class in Oak Park, Illinois, the teacher noticed a girl who looked puzzled and asked her if she had missed the problem. "No," the girl said, "I just can't figure out how my mother did it."

Another teacher brought a Japanese abacus to her fourth grade class to examine in their math center. Soon a very bright boy was using it — as a skateboard!

In Wahiawa, Hawaii, the problem on the board was to subtract 8 from 21. "You can't take 8 away from 1," said the teacher, "because if you had one dog, you couldn't take away 8, could you?" A girl said, "Not unless it was a mother dog."

In New York City, a teacher drew an isosceles triangle on the blackboard and asked a Spanish-speaking boy to name it. The boy absolutely nonplussed the teacher by naming the triangle "Jose."

Overheard in math class: "I hate homework." Second child: "I love homework. It gives me something to do while I watch TV."

In Brooklyn, a teacher was showing the class how to add 2 to 5, but one boy was having difficulty with the idea. "Ask your dad to help you with this tonight," the teacher advised. "It wouldn't be easy for him either," said the boy. The teacher assured him that his father should be able to handle it, and then asked, as an afterthought, "What kind of work does your father do?" "Oh," the boy replied, "he's just an accountant."

The subject of geography is usually introduced to youngsters around the third grade, at an age when they are hardly sophisticated about foreign lands. A boy, asked to name three islands in Indonesia, answered, "Java, Borneo and New Guinea Pig."

A boy in Edwards, New York had an intriguing definition for an island — "A hole in the water that's dry."

A doctor's son in Redondo Beach, California was the only one to raise his hand when the teacher asked what the word "continent" means. He replied, "That's when you can wait until recess to go to the bathroom."

Fourth graders in Tustin, California were studying the Far East. Teacher asked, "Where do the Taiwanese come from?" and a boy answered confidently, "Tijuana." Ole!

All I remember of my biology class is the time we spent dissecting a frog. Yccch! I hated doing it, and I've never ordered frogs' legs in a restaurant since. But in these modern days of rising concern about the ecology, I think it is vital for our kids to study the life sciences and to start developing both understanding and respect for the miracle of life in all its forms on our planet.

I believe children should also be taught how their own bodies work, so they can stay strong and healthy. It's amazing how many grownups know less about their bodies than they do about their cars. And while I realize that sex education is controversial, and I have respect for the good people who argue against it, I do feel some form of sex education is appropriate for our schools. One kid

expressed it perfectly when he said, "I want to know about the sex parts of the body. I don't want to be dirty, I just want the facts."

I'll never forget my own high school days when I dated a sixteen-year-old girl who actually didn't know how babies were conceived. Now, that's serious! In our generation, the schools wouldn't go near the subject of sex — and neither would most parents.

My own children have such a different attitude toward sex than kids of my generation did, because they haven't had to learn about it in the street. There has been very little snickering around our house about it, because it's all been said out in the open, and there is nothing left hidden to laugh or be embarrassed about.

But after reading some of the stories that were sent me about sex education classes, I'm tempted to think that the kids of the seventies don't know much more than we did!

A New York City boy returning from his first day in a fifth grade sex education class reported to his father, "The first thing I learned was that if you laugh you get thrown out."

In New City, New York, a teacher in a maturation program asked her fifth graders if anyone was familiar with the word "puberty."

"Yes," a boy answered. "It is from that old quotation, 'Give me puberty or give me death.' "

A school nurse in Columbiaville, Michigan showed all the fifth grade girls a film on becoming a woman. Next day she asked the girls to write down any

impressions or questions they had about it. One wrote, "It helped me to know more about being a girl . . . only I don't want to go through with it."

Sometimes the kids feel just as awkward in asking about sex as the average teacher does in discussing it. A junior high teacher was interrupted in class by a boy asking, "Would you answer a question about sex?"

"Don't you have a health teacher?" she countered.

"Yes, but I'd rather ask *you.*"

"All right, what is it?"

"I don't have a question right now."

Several days later the same boy approached her with three buddies in the hallway, and asked, "Didn't you say you'd answer any question I had about sex?"

"Yes . . ."

The boy looked triumphantly at his pals. "See? I told you she would!" . . . and walked on down the hall.

In Flushing, New York, two sixth grade classes were following the curriculum for Family Living and Sex Education together. The plan was to view a documentary and then separate the boys and girls for discussions. The movie was about how to care for the skin and avoid acne, but the male teacher allowed the boys to divert him into a topic scheduled for several weeks later.

This became evident when several girls lagged behind class at dismissal and said, "How come the boys have learned about the names of the girl's parts and we're only up to pimples?"

A fifth grade teacher in Brooklyn installed a question box to help make sex education classes more meaningful, and received the following queries that show clearly the lack of knowledge most kids this age have:

"Who teaches dogs and cats how to mate?"

"If you romance longer, is the baby born bigger?"

"Do you think there is a thing like sex even in countries like China?"

"I know that when you intercourse it takes 24 hours. My question is, how do you stay awake?"

When I was in high school, we were never taught a thing about how the human body works, what our internal organs are for and how they function, or anything else about our insides. But doctors tell me I'm in good company, that few adults have any idea of what goes on within their bodies. So it's hardly surprising to see how little our kids know about the human form. One little boy writing about the

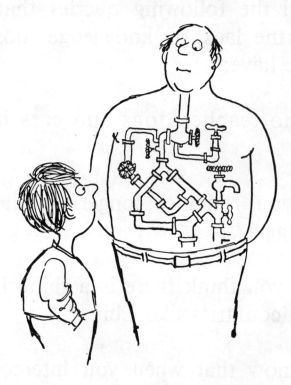

digestive system said, "Food kind of gets slughed around in there. The stumik is connected to the mouth by pipes and stuff. What happens next is . . . To tell the truth, I don't understand this stuff at all. My dad's a plumber, and I asked him why the pipe to the stomik doesn't rust, and he just laughed."

And a boy in Pittsburgh reported that his friend was also hospitalized with "a disussion in his head."

A boy asked to name part of the digestive system wrote, "The large and small contestants."

A girl in Norwich, Connecticut came into class quite upset, explaining that her best friend was going to the hospital "to have her independence cut out."

A kindergartener in Brier, Washington had this health warning for his classmates: "It is important not to be in the sun a long time because the sun stings you. And if it stings you too much, you get wrinkles. And if you get too many wrinkles you will die. My grandmother had a lot of wrinkles and she died."

At the beginning of a first aid class in Coeur d' Alene, Idaho, a girl asked, "Are we going to learn more about mouth-to-mouth suffocation today? If we are, I want to practice on Larry."

Six-year-olds in a Fairfield, Illinois class studied a health book picture of a doctor holding a stethoscope. "What does the doctor have in his hand?" asked the teacher. Little Cathy volunteered: "I'm not sure, but I think it's a thumposcope."

An easy, natural way for kids to learn about biology and the animal world is to have pets. Our youngsters have always had pets of all kinds. When we were living on our ranch in Arizona, we had a succession of calves, rabbits, dogs and horses. One time we went to a cowboy auction and bought three calves. Two became pets, but one of them, a yearling with horns, had a short temper and kept chasing me over the fence — until he ended up in the freezer.

My son Chris had a small Husky dog that did something we thought was amazing — he played with the coyotes. I've never heard of that happening before, but I swear it did. Somehow those wild coyotes accepted him, and he had a lot of fun romping around with them.

As a pet lover, I enjoyed the story of a kindergartener in Straughn, Indiana, who was given permission to show off his new puppy at a faculty meeting. When someone asked whether the puppy was a boy or a girl, the youngster grabbed the pup belly-up and showed it to his mother, who said, "It's a boy." Turning back to the audience, the boy sighed happily. "Isn't she wonderful?" he asked. "She

can tell just by looking at the bottoms of their feet!"

And while we're on the subject of dogs, I can't resist the story of a first grader in Bayside, New Jersey, who was telling his classmates about his new Lhasa Apso puppy. "It has hair all over," he said. "When I hold up a cookie, I never know which end is going to eat it."

Studying domestic animals and their uses, a class in Northridge, California had this exchange with the teacher, who began by asking:

"What animal gives us sausage and bacon?"

"Pigs."

"Where do we get steak?"

"Cows."

"Where do we get lamb chops?"

"Sheep."

"Where do we get hamburger?"

"McDonald's!"

Classes in nutrition are fairly common these days, so most kids know the value of a balanced meal, even if they don't want to eat one.

But when I was a boy, nutrition was never mentioned in the classroom. We didn't learn much about it at home, either. My mom was a big believer in the wonders of cod liver oil. She made me take a teaspoonful of it every day of my young life, and I hated it. The only good part was getting to bite into half an orange after swallowing the awful stuff. Mom also told us we should eat the crusts of our bread, saying that was where all the good nourishment was. I never did figure out how the nourishment crept out of the rest of the bread into the crust like that. She also would urge us to eat burnt toast, because in those days the belief was that burnt toast would make your hair curly. Come to think of it, I ate a lot of that toast, and my hair *is* curly. Maybe she had something there.

Another health-builder that my mother believed in was oatmeal. I ate gallons of the stuff. I remember that when I was five years old she used to serve it in a big bowl that had a picture of a rabbit in the bottom. I couldn't leave the table until that rabbit was staring up at me. I don't have anything against oatmeal today. I realize it's nutritious. But I could never enjoy it now because of all the times I was forced to eat it. For me, emancipation day was when I started to school, and I was allowed the grownup treat of bacon and eggs for breakfast.

A group of second graders in Sumter, South Carolina were told the importance of eating a good breakfast. Then, as

teacher called the roll, she put a star b. the name of each child who reported eating breakfast. When she came to Billy, he hesitated and then said, "I ate breakfast but I threw up. Does that count?"

A first grade girl in Torrance, California came into the nurse's office looking rather pale. Asked if she'd eaten breakfast, the girl answered proudly, "I sure did — made it all myself." "What did you have?" the nurse asked. "A big bowl of maple syrup," the girl said.

After emphasizing the nutritional importance of carbohydrates, proteins and fats, a Brooklyn teacher asked, "Can anyone name the three types of foods necessary for bodily health?"
No one answered for a time until a girl said, "Breakfast, lunch and dinner."

One of the prime topics for the modern health class is a discussion of the hazards of smoking. (That's something else we didn't know about when I was a teen-ager.) As any parent knows, kids just

hate to be lectured, so I like the approach of a teacher in Merrick, New York, who uses humor to get his class to think about the dangers inherent in becoming hooked on cigarettes. I thought you might enjoy what that teacher, Brian Withers, tells his classes. As he says, it sometimes seems that every kid between 16 and 18 carries a cigarette pack as a kind of symbolic badge of defiance.

"I've found that you can't attack the problem head on," he says, "so I've devised a special talk to use whenever smoking comes up." He begins by puffing nervously on a piece of white chalk, and as the kids start to smile, he says, "Many teachers smoke chalk when you're not looking, but they'll never admit it. I'll level with you, though — I do it, and I am proud of it.

"So if you must smoke, don't smoke cigarettes. Try chalk. You can smoke both ends, and no smoke gets in your eyes. You don't need to inhale, and it smells a lot better than cigarettes. You can write with it while you smoke it, so enjoy puffing on a piece while you do your homework. Or

write on someone you like at a party.

"Chalk won't make you cough, or give you cancer or heart disease. Nor will it contribute to emphysema or bronchitis. And it can't cause a fire. You can break it in two — so give your friends a break today. Quit cigarettes and try chalk."

As the teacher finishes, he has a roomful of smiling, laughing, interested kids, all focused in a positive way on the hazards of smoking. As an ex-smoker myself, I can appreciate an imaginative teacher like Brian Withers. So let's chalk one up for him.

Introducing the subject of genetics to a seventh grade class, a teacher in Mexico, Maine mentioned that 23 chromosomes apiece from the father and mother make up the 46 chromosomes of the human fertilized egg cell. An obviously puzzled student asked, "Where does an orphan get his chromosomes?"

A teacher in Pilot Point, Texas explained the life cycle of salmon to his class, describing how the fish battled their

way upstream to lay their eggs and die. A boy commented, "That's what that dumb male gets for chasing that silly female all the way upstream."

A teacher in Yonkers, New York set up a fish tank for his first graders. One morning the children noticed new baby guppies swimming around, and a girl said, "See what happens when you turn the lights off at night?"

As Marshall McLuhan said in that now famous quotation, the entire world is a global village because of electronics. It's commonplace today for teachers to talk of our minds as if they were computers, and vice versa; and the tiniest school children accept television, calculators and other electronic gadgets of the space age as a regular part of their daily lives.

Trying to shush a boy who talked constantly, a Cincinnati teacher said, "You can't seem to keep your mouth closed. I bet you even talk in your sleep."

"No, I don't," the boy replied. "At night I recharge."

A teacher in Pittsburg, Kansas gave some makeup work to a girl who had been absent several days. The girl glanced at one paper and said, "I've already done this. It's a re-run."

Frequently when a child doesn't know an answer, he thinks of something that *seems* to make sense, like the Brooklyn youngster who explained about radios:

"AM radios work in the morning, and FM radios work in the afternoon."

After a science discussion about sound vibrations and how they travel, an alert fourth grader recalled a television story he had seen: "The hunters got off their horses and listened to the ground, trying to find out where the herd of cantaloupe was."

A teacher in Valencia, California was discussing the water cycle with his third graders. Leading up to the idea of condensation, he asked, "Why do you think we have dew on the grass when we wake up in the morning?"
A boy said, "Well, a lot of people walk their dogs at night."

A small boy in Lauderdale Lakes, Florida gave his first science report to his class: "Last night I did an explainament," he said. "I put some water in a dish and this morning it all evominated!"

A teacher in Middletown, Indiana was

trying to impress her first graders that God gave each of them a very special machine inside their heads — their brain. She explained that the machine registers and stores things she said each day, so that they could use the machine to remember the next day when she asked them questions. One morning she asked a boy who was having trouble recalling words, "Where is your little machine this morning?" The boy sighed and said, "I hasn't got it plugged in yet."

In Mt. Kisco, New York, a teacher

described the electron as a particle that had a lot of energy, but was "lazy" and wanted to do as little as possible, settling as close to the nucleus as it could. "You know," a student said, "that electron is a lot like me."

After a science discussion, a Schaumburg, Illinois teacher asked the class to name three atoms, and got this reply from a boy: "Neutrons, protons and croutons."

An eager but inexperienced young science teacher who had done brilliantly in college came into a fourth grade class to invite the children to join in a Science Fair in Oak Park, Illinois. "If you are going to participate, boys and girls," he began, "be sure to bring a card table for your display to the gym. Now as for projects . . . first you will want to choose a subject. For example, through an exhibit, you may answer a question such as, 'Is the force of adhesion between glue and wood more or less than the force of cohesion in wood?' Or perhaps you will want to show

how gears can be used to change the mechanical advantage and direction of a force. Any questions?'' No response. ''Are you sure you understand completely?'' After a few moments a boy in the back row said, ''There's just one thing I'd like to know . . . What's a card table?''

If someone asked me what science I liked best, I wouldn't hesitate a moment. It's astronomy. I never had any particular interest in it as a boy, but when we moved to Arizona and saw that gorgeous sky every night, we just had to have a telescope. I got a big one that was relatively inexpensive, and bought some books to tell me what was up there. Out in Arizona, with the skies so clear, the moon looks as if you could walk on it. (Come to think of it, the astronauts already have.) We could see the rings of Saturn very clearly, too.

I thought of those starry nights in Arizona when I heard about the third grader in Los Angeles who wrote this comment on the discoveries of the space program: "We now know that man cannot live on the other planets. Which shows how smart he was to pick earth in the first place."

Another boy thought that perhaps the scientists were making a mistake in their observatories, saying "Astronomers are looking at the stars with radio waves, but I think they could see lots better with TV waves."

A teacher of fourth graders in La Feria, Texas told the class about an eclipse of the moon that night at ten, suggesting that perhaps their parents would let them stay up late and watch. A boy immediately asked, "Which channel?"

A teacher in Salt Lake City asked her class, "How can astronomers tell the difference between a star and a planet?"

A boy replied, "A star has five points."

In closing this potpourri of science, here are some examination bloopers which show young minds working away, *almost* coming up with the right answers . . .

A boy wrote, "If conditions are not favorable, bacteria go into a period of adolescence."

A girl whose imagination was stronger than her desire to study wrote, "The pistol of a flower is its only protection against insects."

And here are some question and answer exchanges:

Name a prehistoric mammal which was characterized by long upper canine teeth.
"The save a tooth tiger."

Give an example of a disease caused by yeasts.
"Alcoholism."

Describe the food chain.

"A bunch of grocery stores."

What animal has the highest level of intelligence?

"A giraffe."

Name four synthetic fibers.

"Acetate, nylon, rayon and crayon."

And lastly, here are a few other scientific observations you may not have heard until now . . .

"Glass will change shape while in heat."

"Without the law of gravity, people would be afraid to move about for fear they would just fly away."

"One of the most controversial drugs is pot, or, as it is medically known, grass."

How do birds help the farmers?
"They help the farmer to eat the insects."

Describe a Thesaurus.
"I never seen one, but I know they all died a long time ago."

Who founded New York City?
"Christopher Columbus. He was looking for India when he founded us instead."

Strangers in Underwear

As a comedian who once taught Sunday School, I've always found a special delight in the kind of humor that comes bubbling up whenever children first hear about God and religion. The whole notion of God is pretty exciting stuff to kids. The idea of a Supreme Being in charge of the Universe, controlling everything with super powers, isn't too far from the fantasies kids enjoy in the comics or on Saturday morning cartoons.

Not that God is a fantasy; I'm a believer! But when you tell kids that God is all-powerful, knows everything that is going on and what is going to happen, and is everywhere at once, you have just described Someone who has more going for Him in a child's mind than Superman, Wonder Woman and Captain

Marvel combined.

Since the concept of God is so exciting to a child, it would seem that kids would really enjoy Sunday School. Lots of them do, thanks to understanding teachers with a flair for bringing Bible stories to life. But many other kids (and I was among them) have found such classes dull and humdrum. It's that attitude again that some people have about religion having to be so terribly serious, with every sentence sounding like a sermon. I'm all for Sunday School teachers who know a good story and how to tell it. The Bible is crammed with tremendously dramatic stories, as we all know. So why shouldn't the story of David and Goliath, or Daniel in the Lion's Den be as exciting as anything Superman ever did for Lois Lane?

In a parochial school religion period for second graders in Ellisville, Mississippi, the kids were discussing how Jesus lived on earth as part of Joseph's family, and helped him in the carpentry shop. Then the teacher asked, ''Can anyone think of a time in the Bible when Jesus cried?" A girl thought it over and said, "Maybe when he hit his finger with a hammer?"

In Brooklyn, a parochial class was acting out the story of Jesus being tempted by the Devil. The boy playing the Devil told "Jesus," "If you fall down and worship me, all the world will be yours." Jesus looked him defiantly in the eye and said, "Get thee behind me, Satan, and go to Hell."

As you readers have already discovered in these pages, one of the most amusing things about kids is the way they think so literally about ideas that aren't really meant to be exactly what they say. A good example is the first grader in Frederick, Oklahoma who heard the Apostle's Creed for the first time and said, "It seems like God would get mighty tired of Jesus sitting on his right hand."

It was an especially beautiful fall season in Albany, New York, just a few weeks before the national elections, and the

children were all looking out the windows, admiring the colors of autumn. A girl asked the teacher, "Who made all those beautiful colors of nature?" "God did," said the teacher, and the girl said, "I sure hope He runs again this year!"

A visiting psychologist was questioning

some third graders about their ideas of God, asking whether God couldn't be a woman. Interestingly enough, all the boys and girls were in agreement that God was a man. But none of them had reasons for their belief except one very practical young lady who said, "If God was a woman, we'd be saying the 'Our Mother' instead of the 'Our Father.' "

Grown-ups are long accustomed to the idea that two words sounding exactly alike can mean two entirely different things, but a child with a tiny vocabulary frequently trips over the difference. A teacher in Manitowoc, Wisconsin discovered this when she asked her first graders, "For whom did God make the earth?" and a girl said, "The Addams Family."

A second grader in Bristol, Pennsylvania came a cropper in the same way when a nun asked for an example of a bird of prey, and he said, "The Holy Ghost."

In Allentown, Pennsylvania, third

graders were discussing the religion of a classmate who was absent that day. "I think she's a Catholic," said one. "No," said the daughter of a dentist, "she's not. It's something like a Catholic, though. She's a Greek Orthodontist."

On All Saints' Day in Torrance, California, Catholic school, the children were asked to come to school dressed as a favorite saint. Seven-year-old Patrick's mother suggested he go as his namesake, St. Patrick, but the boy objected, saying, "I want to be the saint that liked animals." "Oh," said his mother, "you mean St. Francis of Assisi." The boy looked shocked. "A sissy? Maybe I'd better go as St. Patrick!"

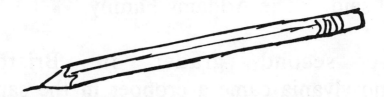

St. Francis is also the central figure in another story sent me by a nun in St. Paul, Minnesota. It seems it was the day of St. Francis, and she was teaching about him because he founded her order. "One hundred and twenty-five years ago," she began, "six women came here from Europe to begin our order in this country." A boy's hand shot up and he asked, "Were you one of them?"

In Royal Oak, Michigan, the nuns had changed their life style and came to school in shortened, modified habits and small veils. A boy looked at one sister and said, "I liked you better in the Old Testament."

In Tacoma, Washington, a mother asked her daughter what she had learned in her first week of attending Sacred Heart Catholic School. The girl thought for a moment and answered, "I learned that nuns aren't really bald-headed, and 'hell' isn't a bad word."

During a Vacation Bible class in Brooklyn, the teacher was talking about John the Baptist as a forerunner of Christ. In summary, she asked, "Who was John the Baptist?" A sophisticated youngster replied, "He discovered Jesus."

Some first graders in a religion class in Oak Park, Illinois were also discussing John, and the sister mentioned that he lived in the desert and ate honey and locusts. "What are locusts?" a girl asked. "Grasshoppers," said teacher. Another girl raised her hand and said, "My grandmother drinks them."

In Martin, Michigan, a teacher of first graders in a small Christian school got a phone call from one of the mothers. "Just what are you teaching those kids?" the woman demanded. "What's wrong?" asked the apprehensive teacher. The mother explained, "My daughter came home and asked me if I knew the Bible song, 'Jesus Wants Me for a Zombie.'"

Two little boys in Palm Springs, California were having a spirited argument about angels. "Angels always have wings," insisted one. "Oh, no," said the other. "My teacher said some of them are strangers in underwear."

The Christmas season frequently brings confusion to light in children's ideas about Santa Claus. A boy in Montrose, California wrote a very forthright note to Santa, saying, "I don't believe in you. I know you're not real because my mom and dad give me the presents. P.S. How do you get the reindeer off the ground?''

In Wheeling, West Virginia, the second graders were discussing Santa and the treats they would put out for him on Christmas Eve. Most of them said they

gave him milk, hot chocolate or coffee, but one girl said, "I find he likes a couple of beers."

Santa Claus was making his annual visit to a school in Barrington, Illinois, talking with all the children. He was asking the usual Santa questions about what the kids wanted from him, when he came to a small boy and said, "Have you been good this year?" "I don't hafta. I'm Jewish," the boy replied.

A teacher in Fort Mitchell, Kentucky recalls a class of second graders in a new suburban private school who were the children of young professional, country club people. She was telling them how Mary and Joseph traveled to Bethlehem, and found there was no room at the inn. Attempting to combine a language and a religious lesson, she assigned the class to write letters inviting Mary and Joseph to stay with them. One letter she will always cherish said, "Dear Mary and Joseph, Next time you are in Bethlehem, stop in and have a drink with us."

In Des Moines, a teacher asked the kids to write anonymous letters about what they did to please their mothers at Christmas. She began reading aloud such replies as, "I made her a cutting board" . . . "I helped her make place cards" . . . and then was astonished to read, "I gave my mother a mink coat." She looked around the class and a boy said, "Well, it was really my brother and I who gave her the coat — but I couldn't spell 'corduroy.' "

The moment of truth for many a teacher is when she asks the class a key question about their studies. After reviewing Middle East history, a Bronx high school teacher asked a boy to name three contributions of the Early Hebrews. "Let's see," he hesitated. "There's monotheism . . . the Old Testament . . . and kosher salami."

During a lesson on the part the Mormons played in America's westward movement, a fifth grade teacher in Royal

Oak, Michigan explained polygamy as the practice of having more than one wife at a time. But after revealing that Brigham Young, an important church leader who led the Mormons to Utah, had 27 wives, she noticed a puzzled look on a boy's face.

"What's wrong, Jason?" she asked. "Don't you understand the meaning of polygamy?"

"Yes," he said, "but I was just wondering how they all got into the same bed."

Quite often when a child doesn't know an answer, he will use his imagination to come up with something plausible, just as we adults do. A class in Fairbury, Nebraska was studying parts of the Mass, and the pastor asked, "Why do we call Christ 'the Lamb of God'?" A boy thought about it and replied, "I guess so we can sing that song, 'Mary Had a Little Lamb.' "

A teacher in an Albuquerque parochial school remembers escorting two older boys back to class after confession. As they were coming down the church steps, they began arguing heatedly. Finally one said in exasperation, "If I wasn't in the state of grace, I'd sock you. Just you wait 'til I get out of it!"

The publishers hope that this Large Print Book has brought you pleasurable reading. Each title is designed to make the text as easy to see as possible. G. K. Hall Large Print Books are available from your library or local bookstore or through the Large Print Book Club. If you would like a complete list of the Large Print Books we have published or information about our Book Club, please write directly to:

G. K. Hall & Co.
70 Lincoln Street
Boston, Mass. 02111